Beneath the Guiding Light

An interesting insight into the
history of the Withernsea Lighthouse
and the surrounding town.

by
Victoria Allott

Santona Publications
Hull
2001

Beneath The Guiding Light

First Published in 2001

Cover Photograph of Withernsea Lighthouse
by Victoria Allott

British Library Cataloguing-in-Publication Data.
A catalogue record for this book is available from the British Library.

Copyright © 2001 by Victoria Allott.

Victoria Allott is hereby identified as the author of this work in accordance with Section 77 of the Copyright, Designs and Patents Act of 1988.

First Published in 2001 by;
Santona Publications, Hull.

All rights reserved. No part of this publication may be reproduced or transmitted in any form or by any means, electronic or mechanical, including photocopy, recording, or any information storage or retrieval system, without permission in writing from the publishers.

Printed by The Amadeus Press, West Yorkshire.

ISBN 0 9538448 1 1

Acknowledgements

Many thanks to our sponsors, without whom this venture would not have been possible:

British Gas
B. P.
The Withernsea Community Chest
Consignia
The Friends of the Lighthouse
The Lighthouse Trustees
Project 2000
Withernsea Town Council

We are extremely grateful to you all for your generous donations.

The author would also like to personally thank the following for their endless support and numerous hours of proofreading:

Janet Standley
Jim and Joy Drewery
James Maxwell
Chris Hughes
The Friends of the Lighthouse
The Lighthouse Trustees

It couldn't have been done without you!

And last but definitely not least, many thanks to Jules and John for their brilliant taxi service during the disaster of January. What a great way to start a year!

Beneath The Guiding Light

Contents

Introduction. The Journey Begins.	Page 6
1. The Railway Arrives.	Page 9
2. The 'Pier Craze'.	Page 14
3. The Guiding Light.	Page 18
4. Braving the Seas Fury.	Page 24
5. From the Highest Heights to the Deepest Depths.	Page 30
6. The Legend of Will O' Withernsea.	Page 39
7. It's Time to Learn.	Page 43
8. Fame at Last.	Page 49
9. Films, Films, Films.	Page 56
10. All the Fun of the Fair.	Page 58
Bibliography.	Page 64

Introduction

The Journey Begins

The Withernsea Lighthouse was built after the tragedy of the "Genesta," to reduce the number of shipwrecks that fell prey to the hazardous coastline. During its working life it prevented hundreds of disasters. It was finally made redundant in the year of 1976 when modern technology had succeeded the Lighthouse's capabilities. It remained derelict until it was purchased by Dr Rolla and Kim Campbell who transformed it into a museum in memory of Kim's sister, Kay Kendall, a famous Hollywood actress of the 1950's, who sadly died of leukaemia at the youthful age of 32. The museum is now a registered charity, run by a board of trustees, and all proceeds from this book will be donated towards this worthwhile cause.

Echoes of the Lighthouse: The Lighthouse's Story

So there I was at last, a much needed and long awaited Lighthouse at Withernsea.

An octagonal tower tapering 127ft high, 144 steps and a gold weathervane on top. Pretty impressive.

They had taken 18 months to complete my specifications as set out by Trinity House and built me a quarter of a mile from the eroding shore.

During the building the echo reverberated with the workmen's voices inside the tower, "Genesta" said the echo, "One of hundreds of ships lost, hundreds of ships lost."

I had been erected here to stop the endless tragedy of wrecks along this hostile coastline.

There was no grand opening ceremony, as you might have expected, and they were 3 whole weeks balancing my lens in 3 gallons of mercury before they got the sequence of light right.

Come to think of it, the locals would have been quite frightened when it first shone; I can remember them coming out into the streets to see what it was all about.

Every Lighthouse has its own characteristic light signal. Mine was special. Two short flashes and one long sweeping beam which lit up bedroom windows and then spread over the sea, reassuring the passing ships they were on the right course.

My two cottages were occupied by the keepers and their families, and a relief came for holidays.

They kept me in pristine condition. The turn of the lens was timed each night with a stopwatch and the clockwork mechanism was rewound every

Introduction

day. All my brass was clean and sparkling and the sun-lit faces of my tower stood out proudly against the skyline.

All was well and time moved on. There was a bit of a commotion when my light was electrified and my character was changed to a single white flash every 3 seconds. Despite this advance in technology the keepers still kept a backup of umpteen bulbs, batteries, paraffin and a standby generator.

Together we never failed or faltered. During the Second World War my light was covered, only drawing back the curtain to guide the Convoys on their dangerous missions.

One day the keeper didn't climb the stairs to the service room for his usual shift. He must be ill, I thought. I waited. Must be serious. The assistant keeper didn't come, nor the relief. Very strange. The afternoon drew on and by sunset I was getting rather anxious. What about my light! What about the ships! We could not fail them. What would the people think, what would they say!

No-one ever came that day, my light did not shine, and it never shone again.

After a while the workmen came to take the lens away, my beautiful lens all dismantled. "Going to St. Mary's" said the echo "At Whitley Bay, At Whitley Bay."

There I was, deserted, forgotten, how could they forget? I was damp and cold. My light had gone out, all my brass had tarnished and the paint had started to peel from the walls of my tower.

I couldn't believe it - my heart was breaking - all we had together, all the lives we had saved. "Not wanted" said the echo. "Modern Technology, Made Redundant, Made Redundant."

I began to wonder - if they had taken the lens, would they decide to dismantle my bricks? - The whole building? Heaven forbid!

It was the banging and clattering that shook me that morning. It was the workmen again, oh no! Arriving in trucks and vans carrying wood and plasterboard this time.

The tower was startled with the echo "Been sold," it said. "We'll make a Museum, make a Museum." The words were lost in the hub of activity. Over the weeks the name "Kay Kendall" drifted up the stairs "Film star, Film Star," I was once a star I thought - could she shine for me?

Today I am the Withernsea Lighthouse Museum, Registered Charity with a Board of Trustees. Pretty impressive.

I am newly painted inside and out, and I understand I am one of the biggest tourist attractions in Holderness, with some 6000 visitors each season

Beneath the Guiding Light

coming to see me. They wander through the Museums rooms which are filled with Lifesaving equipment and pictures and models of the old town, of the railway and the hospital, as they used to be. Then there is the Memoriam to Kay, Film Star, Withernsea's child, born to be famous, yet dying, oh so young.

"Only 12 at a time! says the echo, "Be careful on the stairs, be careful" as parties of school children wait excitedly to climb to the top, always remembering the experience.

I have a caretaker now who helps to keep me well maintained. I also have a loyal band of volunteers, without whose help I could not stand proudly again. Although my heart came near to breaking, I'm happy now, loved and cared for. "Enjoy," says the echo, "Enjoy, enjoy."

('Echoes of the Lighthouse' written by Janet Standley).

Chapter 1

The Railway Arrives

The Withernsea railway owes its success to one man, Anthony Bannister. Originally a Hull fish merchant, ship owner and exporter, Bannister continually played an active public role. In 1845 he became the town councillor for the North Myton ward before serving Hull as Sheriff in both 1849 and 1850. Bannister, renowned for entering public life with energy and zeal became Mayor for the first time in 1851 and was made an alderman in 1855.

It was during his time serving as Mayor that Bannister first envisaged the possibility of a railroad running through South Holderness. Aware that it would provide the ideal opportunity of capturing the beef and corn trade, the businessman saw the money making potential of transporting cattle and grain to the markets of Hull and even further afield. He also aspired to create a thriving tourist town, thus assuming the railway projected eastwards from Patrington to the coast, it seemed possible to create a seaside resort the quality of Bridlington or Scarborough. Withernsea was the perfect site for this dream, it had all the advantages to make it a perfect terminus; the lack of vast stretches of cliffs meant that the thousands of excited tourists visiting the resort could easily reach the beach, the sea wall reduced erosion - limiting its potential to become a highly destructive force, and finally, if a pier was built it would not only attract more customers but could also be used as a landing site for fish, which could then be sent directly to Hull via the railroad. This was Bannister's dream, his plans, both elegant and ambitious, were too much for one man to fulfil, hence a committee was formed calling itself the 'Hull and Holderness Railway Company.' The officials shared Bannister's ambitious zeal and had high hopes for the quiet, agricultural village of Withernsea. Together, they had visions of a grand station hotel, boulevards, promenades, crescents, tree lined avenues and assembly halls. Withernsea was to be the Filey of the future. In addition to this they were aware that the railway would prove invaluable to local farmers, thus little resistance would be put forward to oppose their plans.

September 1852 saw the issue of the prospectus for the 'Hull and Holderness Railway Co.' and although costly, Bannister encountered no problems in raising the share capital of £153,000. The 'Hull and Holderness Railway Act' received Royal Assent on the 8th July 1853 and work began on the construction of the line, nothing could stop him now. Contractors agreed to complete the line for a fee of £67,000, excluding the stations and gatehouses, and on the 6th December 1853 an estimate for the total cost was recorded in the Board's minutes at £100,000, including £6,000 for Hull Station and works, and £1,000 for the Withernsea Station and works.

9

Beneath the Guiding Light

To add to the already excessive costs, Hull's local architect, Cuthbert Brodrick, was employed by Bannister to build an imposing Station Hotel at Withernsea, complete with 40 bedrooms, ladies drawing room, elegant coffee room, billiard and smoke room, baths and lawn tennis ground. This grey brick hotel was 3 storeys high and 11 bays long, it also had a dancing saloon and in total this venture cost £10,530. It opened on the 12th April 1855 when its name was changed to the Queens Hotel. This event was celebrated with a ball, and the music for the occasion included 5 pieces entitled 'The Withernsea Quadrilles' by Enderby Jackson, all of which were dedicated to Bannister who had become Mayor of Hull for the second time.

To celebrate the opening of the railway, a luncheon was held, the guests, amounting to 500 in total, were issued with tickets for its first ever journey which was set to leave Paragon Station at 11am. However, as is often the case with public transport, the train was 20 minutes late in leaving the station, not through any fault concerning Bannister's organisation, but simply because some guests had not arrived on time. Sadly, the weather took a turn for the worst and it began to rain, luckily the celebration luncheon at Withernsea was held in a marquee enabling a great feast to be had by all despite the dreary weather, until, that was, nearly one third of the marquee collapsed due to the stormy conditions and a broken rope. The forgiving guests were swiftly re-seated and the celebrations recommenced.

Before the opening of the railway in the 1850's there is no evidence that visitors were attracted to Withernsea. It was only a small village with a slowly rising population, a total of 76 inhabitants in 1801, a number which had risen to 108 by 1821. Although a few of these families were employed in trade, the main source of income was through agriculture, thus the town was not an initial tourist magnet. And although by 1840 the village had an inn, the Sailors Return, now known as the Commercial, it was not until the opening of the railway in 1854, that the small village rapidly developed into a fully fledged town, rich with possibilities of future development.

A staggering 63,764 passengers travelled to Withernsea in the four months following the 17th July 1854, the town appeared to be flourishing and Bannister's dream seemed well within reach. Yet this early success was not sustained, and it soon became evident that the railway was unprofitable. This was partly caused by the single line track from Hull to Withernsea which drastically reduced the flow of people, yet to ensure the safety of the passengers only one train at a time was permitted to travel on the track. Hence, it came as no surprise that on the 1st January 1860 the unprofitable 'Hull and Holderness

The Railway Arrives

Railway Co.' was leased to the 'North Eastern Railway' (NER) and two years later, on the 7th July 1862, an Act of Parliament dissolved Bannister's company. In an attempt to amend this serious lack of viability, a second track was built and laid by the NER, a company which continued to control the Hull to Withernsea railway for a further 60 years.

During the years in which the railway was under the control of the NER, the town of Withernsea, once a small agricultural village, expanded into a popular tourist resort. People flocked to the coast in their thousands, leaving behind the smog and stench of the industrial cities. At first it was only the affluent who could afford to stay in the town, but shortly afterwards, when the locals realised that there was money to be made in the tourist trade, everyone with a room to spare began to take in visitors, charging more reasonable rates than the excessively priced Queens Hotel. The commuter age had begun and the railway could now afford to offer cheap day return tickets, as a result of this day trips became more accessible to the less affluent. Many returned each year while others, who saw the profitability of the town, decided to set up residence. Needless to say, a few boarding houses shortly lined the coast.

But sadly, by this time the control of the railway was no longer in the hands of Bannister, whose ambition to breathe life into the town had been highly successful. Nevertheless, Bannister remained faithful to the town and in 1870 he turned his ambitions towards another beneficial scheme 'The Withernsea Pier, Promenade, Gas and General Improvement Company.' So, along with 6 other directors and a registered capital of £40,000, Bannister was again in business. Endeavouring to reduce erosion along the coastline, five groynes were built by the company, and the 1872 prospectus highlighted yet again, the issue which was close to Bannister's heart, it spoke of negotiations with the NER for the provision of daily express trains for the convenience of Withernsea commuters to Hull. It also outlined plans to build a promenade and a pier. With Bannister's efficiency it comes as no surprise to discover that by 1873 part of the North Promenade was finished and in 1877 the pier had been completed. The year afterwards Bannister died, however, the improvement company lived on and his position as chairman was taken over by James Young, a local man. Yet the 'Improvement Company' experienced the same fate as the railway and shortly it ran out of money, its final act being to purchase the Queens Hotel from the NER in 1881. The following year the company went into liquidation.

Although Bannister's grand dreams faded with the demise of the 'Improvement Company' his spirit lived on in the local people, who, having

Beneath the Guiding Light

already witnessed the rapid transformation of their town, took a personal interest and began to propose increasingly modest plans. With the inspiration Bannister provided and the commitment of the hard working local people, success was not far away. The population of the town was increasing at a faster rate than ever, by 1901 the population had risen to 1,426, in 1911 it was 2,384 and by 1921 a staggering total of 4,701 people resided in the town.

Despite the removal of the remaining 50ft of the pier in 1903, Withernsea still had the ability to attract visitors. The passing years saw the gradual accumulation of leisure facilities, thus Withernsea, with a bandstand and assembly rooms within which all forms of entertainment would take place, an open air swimming pool, a cricket and tennis club, as well as a handful of cinemas, had the amenities to provide for the ever increasing crowds of tourists. By 1914 there were approximately 13 trains running daily between Hull and Withernsea, even more unusual is the fact that they also ran on Sundays. Employees of Reckitt and Sons financed outings for the poor children of Hull to many places, one of these was Withernsea, 3,000 children had participated in this scheme by the year of 1923. The company also ran a separate old folk's scheme and by 1962 3,594 pensioners had been taken to Withernsea.

Yet the 'hey days' of the railway were not to last forever and one of the first blows occurred in the early 1920's with the introduction of a local bus service. The road from Hull to Withernsea was surfaced with tarmac and the official brochure released in 1926 claimed that "the Automobile Association

Above. Railway Fever struck and thousands of people flocked to Withernsea.

The Railway Arrives

had now certified the road to be good." However, the railway continued to plod on until 1960 when its deficit could no longer be ignored. Its annual earnings were £37,000 yet the annual direct costs had reached £78,000, its financial struggle was obvious. In 1963 Dr Richard Beeching, who had been asked by the government to produce a blueprint which would return rail travel to profitability, published his conclusive report which held the fate of the Withernsea line in its grip. The report entitled 'The Reshaping of British Railways' suggested the elimination of one third of the rail network, among the suggested closures was the Hull to Withernsea line. Beeching pointed out that the railway had never been profitable and by 1962 it was losing money at a rate of £41,000 per year. The local people were enraged at the suggestion of closure and an official notice claimed that objections should be lodged at the Grand Pavilion on the 6th January 1964. The response, although unbelievable, served only to prolong the life of the line for a short while. On the 19th October 1964 the residents of Withernsea witnessed the final journey of the towns passenger train, their sadness symbolised by a wreath which was placed on the end of the buffers. Thus the railway, in many cases the secret formula of the towns initial success, ended its 110 year life. Now all that can be seen of the once popular railway is the rough cinder track leading to Patrington.

Until recently, the open-air market which operated on the station platform attracted many day-trippers to the town. Pessimists believed that the decline of the railway would result in the decline of the town, yet the increase in public transport meant that the effects were not as devastating as first predicted. However, those who remember the railway still recall the delights and convenience of the short journey through Holderness, without the hassle of traffic problems along the way. Even those who do not remember the railway cannot help but feel somewhat indebted to the steam powered giant which helped to transform the small agricultural village of yesteryear into the friendly tourist town we have grown to know and love today.

Chapter 2

The 'Pier Craze'

The 'pier craze' took place in the first half of the 18th Century and owes it's popularity to Sir John Floyer and Dr Richard Russel. The pair claimed that drinking sea water was a miracle cure for many illnesses ranging from rheumatism and ulcers to the more serious ailments of cancer and deafness. Shortly after the release of this theory, doctors and physicians from far and wide were prescribing the practice of sea bathing, as well as further advice for people to take a break from the smog and congestion of industrial cities by travelling to the coast to breathe in the health giving sea air. Piers provided people with the perfect opportunity of doing this without the hassle of accessing a boat or the additional worry of seasickness.

Again the ambitious alderman Anthony Bannister seized the opportunity to fulfil his dream and turn Withernsea into a major seaside resort. He was aware that a pier was an essential addition to the resort if it was to attract more visitors to the town and so in 1871 he formed the 'Withernsea Pier, Promenade, Gas and General Improvement Company.' When the company issued its prospectus the following year, it came as no surprise to discover that it included the blueprint for a pleasure pier situated at the north end of the town. However, shortly after the designs were drawn up they were abandoned in favour of a new pier which was to be located opposite the railway station. The year of 1875 saw Bannister's plan put into action when work on the pier was started.

Bannister harboured silent hopes that the pier with its saloon would not only reach out and embrace the holiday spirit of the Victorian middle-class, but may also have a commercial angle to it's future. It was proposed that Withernsea had the potential to become a fishing port, with North Sea vessels using the pier to land their catches for transportation to Hull by rail, thereby saving valuable time. Unfortunately for Bannister, technology advanced making his plans obsolete, as access to the Humber was no challenge to the new steam trawlers.

Whilst under construction, the pier suffered some storm damage, which some claimed to be an omen representing the future struggles the pier was to face. Yet this small setback only slightly inhibited progress and work on the pier was completed in August 1877. The following year the £12,000 pier was officially opened. People came from miles around to view the construction of timber decking and iron girders all supported by delicate cast iron piles which were screwed into the beach. No expense was spared, seating ran along the

The 'Pier Craze'

length of the pier for added comfort and at the end of the pier a Saloon was situated. At the entrance stood a large brick castellated gateway to welcome visitors to the huge attraction, this was apparently modelled on Conway Castle and was nicknamed 'The Sandcastle.' To ensure stability, the foundations of this magnificent gateway were embedded in the clay, a tunnel was also dug beneath them which ran to an exit door on the beach to enable maintenance work to take place. Nothing escaped Bannister's attention, or at least, that's how it seemed to begin with.

Entrance to the pier was charged at 1 penny, and for the first two years of its life the pier was a great success - especially with the large numbers of day-trippers from Hull who arrived by rail. During this prosperous time the 'Pier Company' made a small profit. However, the initial success was short lived and it wasn't long before disaster struck, leaving a succession of devastation in its wake.

The first blow to the pier took place on the night of the 28th October 1880. The town watched in horror as a fierce storm thundered along the Yorkshire coast, damaging any vessels that attempted to brave its rage. During that night the pier was struck by two storm damaged vessels. The 'Jabez' was the first to strike, it collided with the end of the pier and sank. Later that night a second attack took place, this time it was the turn of the snow 'Saffron' which punched a 200ft hole through the middle of the pier. The pier was rapidly repaired although timber was used instead of iron, this fatal mistake ensured that the stormy sea which began to swell on the night of the 28th March 1882 was powerful enough to wash away the pier head and its Saloon. These were never replaced.

As is often the case, a period of calm emerged after the storm and the pier continued to stand tall until 20th October 1890 when, as a result of a storm damaged vessel, the pier was reduced vastly to a length of 300ft. The dramatic event occurred when the Grimsby fishing smack 'Genesta' was forced to run aground nearby Waxholme on the previous evening. Fortunately, the boat was unscathed and the crew escaped with the exception of the captain who, during his attempt to regain control of the vessel, froze to the rigging and died. The next morning the budding businessmen of the town auctioned the boat and sold it. However, whilst the new owner sat smugly brooding over his bargain buy another storm drove the unmanned 'Genesta' along the coast to Withernsea until it crashed into the pier, destroying more than half of it. Fate holds it that one bad event is always rivalled by a good event and this case was no exception to the rule. At the inquest of 'Genesta's' captain the coroner

Beneath the Guiding Light

Withernsea's famous boating lake was a popular crowd pleaser. In the background the 'Pier Towers' stand tall and proud.

The 'Pier Craze'

claimed that he believed the tragedy could have been avoided if a guiding light had been present at Withernsea. As a result of this the lighthouse was built, work was started early in 1893.

Unfortunately the lighthouse arrived too late to rescue the pier from its disastrous fate. At 9 o' clock on the night of the 22nd November 1893 a large barque, named the 'Henry Parr'(formerly known as 'Dido'), which had been drifting off the Withernsea coastline came ashore. At 11 o' clock the vessel, beaten and battered, broke into pieces and began to approach the pier at a rate of 7 or 8 miles per hour. Within half an hour the boat struck, taking with it deals and fencing rails, which, in some places, were littered up to 10 feet high. The pier's final hour arrived as the wreckage came into contact with the piles of the pier, it ripped them down displaying a triumphant spray of sparks as it drifted along. After this final attack a feeble 50ft of the pier remained, this survived until 1903 when it was removed during reconstruction work on the sea wall.

Now after the merciless attack of the sea, all that remains of the pier is the castellated twin towered gateway which was once the pier entrance. The memory of it survives in its name, the 'Pier Towers,' which, although serves as an emotional memory of the piers demise, clings to nostalgic memories of happier days. Although the pier was demolished the towers continued to serve the community in a variety of ways. Not only were they used as a backdrop for the famous pierrot shows, but, more recently, the north tower has been used as a beach masters office and as a base for St John's Ambulance, whilst the south tower was a penny bazaar gift shop and later became home to the coastguard station which has now relocated to a new building adjacent to the promenade.

Chapter 3

The Guiding Light

Over the passing centuries the hazardous 57 mile stretch of coastline between the lighthouses of Spurn and Flamborough has become the silent resting place for thousands of vessels. During the 19th Century it was considered a praiseworthy achievement for a vessel to pass safely along the stretch. The loss of ships was such a frequent occurrence that only the large ones have been recorded. However, after the tragedy of the 'Genesta' it was decided that Withernsea needed a lighthouse and in 1892 Trinity House purchased a half acre piece of land with this venture in mind. This parcel of land was part of the Enholme Pasture owned by Emma Swann, widow of Samuel Swann, and stood along Hull Road just one quarter of a mile inland. Many people find the distance from the shore one of the most unusual features about the lighthouse, however, considering the weakness and instability of the clay cliffs the lighthouse would have stood little chance of survival if situated directly on the coastline, probably falling into the sea even before its construction was complete!

Work began immediately and anyone who was prepared to put in a day's hard work for a reasonable wage would go and help to dig the foundations. During the winter the weather was so bad that local fisherman, Bob Drewery (later to be the Grandfather of Terry, Kim and Kay Kendall), was unable to launch his boat upon which his livelihood depended, so throwing down his casting nets and picking up his shovel he joined the numerous locals and went to help with the digging. Bob was always proud to claim that he was "the only man to have been under the lighthouse, in it and over it." It is quite amusing to ponder for a moment upon the images conjured up by the minds of people who didn't understand what he meant. Not only did Bob help to dig the foundations, he also took advantage of an offer made to him by a pioneering pilot who, when a bit strapped for cash, offered to take Bob up in his plane for a fee of 5 shillings, thus Bob Drewery flew over the lighthouse.

The lighthouse took approximately 18 months to build and the light first shone on the 1st March 1894. Many people were ecstatic, this new guiding beam would ensure that their coastline was no longer riddled with corpses and wreckages that had all fallen victim to the treacherous coastline. Others were not so happy, this new giant that towered over the town frightened them with its intruding beam. The clash of interests resulted in riots and many livelihoods were ruined as the ever decreasing number of wrecks littering the coastline meant people could no longer make their living by salvaging goods from the ruins. However, the lighthouse continued to stand tall and remained loyal to the townsfolk.

The Guiding Light

The lighthouse's structure is of brick and concrete, according to the Trinity House tradition, its octagonal walls are 5 feet thick and many find its shape architecturally unusual. Its foundations are 15 feet deep and it stands 127 feet high. It has always been white, with black slate roof dwellings. There are 144 steps to the light room and on top of the lighthouse sits a wind vane in the form of a golden arrow. This is connected to a compass which can be seen on the ceiling of the light room.

When the lighthouse first opened the original light was an 8 wick paraffin lamp which was situated within an octagonal revolving lens with a bulls eye on each side. During the day these bulls-eye lenses were a potential fire hazard as they could concentrate the suns rays to such an intensity that it was possible to cause fires at ground level, hence operating like a magnifying glass. As a result of this the lens would be covered up during the day to protect it from the sun, in addition to this a steel curtain covered the landward side of the light so that it did not shine over the town.

The lens, weighing 2 tons, was floated on a trough of 3 gallons of mercury which, despite its weight, meant that it could be moved by the slightest touch. It was turned by the action of a two-hundredweight weight which was suspended down the centre of the tower. This was timed each evening by a stopwatch to ensure that the regular rhythm of 24 seconds for a complete turn was maintained. Thus, each flash was in synch with each bulls-eye giving a sweep of light every three seconds. On a clear night the light reached a distance of up to 17 miles. However, in the case of bad visibility such as fog, the light was exhibited 1 hour before sunset and until 1 hour after sunrise, instead of the usual sunset to sunrise schedule.

The upkeep of the lighthouse was a monotonous task. The strict routine of chores was rigidly adhered to, including the clockwork controlling mechanism of the light, which required winding daily to bring the weight to the top. This gave the system turning power for 14 hours. In addition to this, the glazing was cleaned regularly by syringe method. Water to fill the syringe was obtained, by bucket, from a rainwater tank in the service room. The brass ventilators and handrails were polished frequently, this was a time consuming job considering the numerous ventilators required in the lamp room to reduce the condensation, a prominent problem in lighthouses. Furthermore, the watches were split into two shifts, the first was from 11pm until 4am and the second was from 4am until noon. The remaining hours were shared by the principle lighthouse keeper and his assistant with very little free time. During the watches, records of the weather had to be noted, details on conditions and

Beneath the Guiding Light

visibility levels were entered into the book every three hours, the watchers used the compass on the ceiling of the lamp room to aid them in their research. Originally there were two lighthouse keepers, namely Mr W. J. Rees and Mr W. Robins who resided in the house and cottage attached to the lighthouse

The year of 1936 saw the light electrified when the paraffin lamp was replaced by a 100 volt, 1500 watt bulb, supplied from the main grid. This resulted in the range being increased from 17 miles to 25 miles on a clear night. The bulbs have a similar appearance to the standard house bulb, the only difference being that they measure 18ins in length and have a circumference of 16ins. There was a back up plan to ensure that all ran smoothly in the event of bulb failure, in this case a second bulb would automatically move into its place and, should the main electricity fail, a third bulb lit by a bank of 26 rechargeable batteries would serve as a final resort. A standby generator was also provided for emergency use. Yet, in the unlikely event of total failure of all three alternatives, an old faithful paraffin lamp was retained in reserve.

Sadly, in 1970 Trinity House began closing down lighthouses. Technology had advanced and superseded the old-fashioned lighthouses, as navigational aids both ashore and afloat began to cast doubt on the necessity for shore lights. On the 1st July 1976, the light shone for the last time and the lighthouse stood alone and unwanted. However, it was bought by Kim Campbell and resurrected in the form of a museum in memory of her sister Kay Kendall, a Withernsea born girl, who hit Hollywood fame in the 1950's. And yet, although the lighthouse is no longer in operation, the following extract provides a perfect summary of daily life in the working lighthouse:

Report by 'Special Commissioner' "A Snug Lighthouse by the Sea"
"Entering the lighthouse through the corridor connecting it with the houses of the keepers, I was struck by the simplicity of the interior. You see right up to the floor of the one little room the lighthouse contains, perched immediately below the lantern. It is, as I have said, a shell - something of a telescope on end with gracefully tapering sides. Stone stairs run round, circular stairs, but of a good 'tread', and quite easy to mount if you can forget their number. The walls of the lighthouse are tremendously thick, 5 feet 6, I think I was told, at the base. They are built of a particular kind of brick, but massively concreted outside and in, practically as good as stone and quite as weather tight...Withernsea is one of the tallest lights upon the coast, and in the peculiarity of its position - at the back of a sea town, or village - it is only rivalled by a light at South Wold, in Sussex.

The Guiding Light

The Lighthouse is situated on Hull Road. Many visitors to the town find it unusual that the lighthouse should be so far inland!

Beneath the Guiding Light

A popular postcard illustrating some of the town's more memorable features

The Guiding Light

About 15 gallons of oil are needed each night in winter and thick weather, in clear weather and summer a smaller quantity will be used.

At Withernsea there is an 8-wick lamp, and the outer wicks are of a wide circumference. When all are lit the glass chimney is filled by about a foot or more, of fiercely glowing white flame. The heat is intense, but is carried off, in great measure, by a new pattern of iron chimney descending upon the glass chimney that protects the flame. In clear weather the outer wicks are set alight, and the lamp is then worked at half power. In thick weather the whole blaze their white warning far across the waters. There are two lamps fixed within the powerful irradiators, condensers, and reflectors - great glasses, very brittle, very brilliant in their whiteness - arranged to shoot the lamp's rays into the night. One lamp is lit in the evening, and kept burning till midnight, then the other is lit, and by a swivel arrangement is placed in the centre, the first lamp swinging out of the way. To make the change, re-connect the taps and turn on the oil only takes 30 seconds - a smart bit of business. The light is a flashing one, a great iron cylinder descending and hiding the flame for 3 seconds; then ascending for 3 seconds, again dark for 3 seconds, light for 3 seconds, dark for 3 seconds, finally light for 45 seconds - completing the minute. The cylinder is very ingeniously worked by a series of weights and pendulum. The flashes are timed - accurately. The clockwork is wound up every hour; but it will work faithfully for 2 hours at a stretch."

Chapter 4

Braving the Sea's Fury

The year of 1824 witnessed the beginning of a service which was to save the lives of thousands in years to come. The National Lifeboat Institution or 'NLI' was a valuable charity founded by Sir William Hillary and dependant upon donations for it's survival. Now known as the RNLI or the Royal National Lifeboat Institution, the service continues to show the dedication which has always brought it much praise.

It didn't take long for the charitable concept to sweep throughout the country and as the donations slowly increased the NLI was able to improve its service. In 1862, the dedicated lifeboat men of Withernsea received their first boat, it was donated by Miss Sara Lechmere, a clergyman's daughter, and was christened 'Pelican' in correspondence with the family crest. To house the £300 lifeboat a boathouse was built in Arthur Street, this is now more commonly known as the Social Services office. The boat was 34 feet long, 7 feet wide and could be rowed 6 oars single banked and 12 oars double banked. Many were proud of the boats valuable qualities; not only did it have great lateral stability, but it had the added value of speed against a heavy sea, it's ability to rapidly discharge water aided this. It was fully facilitated to launch and take to sea, with self-righting properties if it was upset. But probably the most essential qualities it had were strength and its ability to carry a large number of passengers.

The launching of the lifeboat on the 28th August 1862 was a huge event, the town had never witnessed such a great celebration. Crowds were drawn from far and wide to witness the joyous occasion, and even though arrangements for the provision of extra trains were made, this was still not enough to suffice the excessive crowds. The demand for transport was so high that excursionists reached the town in whatever way they could. Many travelled on the fire steamer 'Zebra,' which was decorated for the ceremony accordingly. The steamer left the Corporation Pier at Hull sporting a magnificent 400 passengers, and after a four hour trip the revellers reached Withernsea. The boats owner rapidly slipped into the celebratory mood, donating all takings towards the costs of the days proceedings. There was such demand to witness the ceremony that people travelled from Hull on yachts and sailing boats, those who couldn't afford this were not put off, travelling by horse and carriage or even walking. An estimation suggests that 20,000 people turned out for the ceremonious launch.

While the anxious crowds gathered, the boat remained in the boathouse, silently resting on its carriage. Slowly a large procession trundled through

Braving the Sea's Fury

the town, making its way towards the hut, all were anxious to catch a glimpse of the magnificent boat. By 4pm the procession had begun, starting with a prayer from the Reverend G. C. Pearse of Paull. Afterwards, manned by its 15 strong crew, the lifeboat, drawn by 8 horses, began its journey towards the beach. The men, standing tall and proud upon the boat displayed their cork lifebelts and were followed on foot by their wives, recognisable by their neat white caps.

Upon reaching the sands, the boat was christened by Miss Champney, who, whilst throwing a bottle of wine at the boat proclaimed "I name this boat Pelican, God speed her." Afterwards the lifeboat set sail where it was to demonstrate its self-righting properties, a much needed facility if it was to brave the waves.

Whilst the celebrations flared, all attendants were unaware of the valuable service the lifeboat would provide. During its 15 years of service, the 'Pelican' was launched 13 times and saved 42 lives. Its first launch took place on the 27th April 1864. The dilemma was triggered early one Saturday morning when some fishing boats set off to haul up their lines which had been laid the previous afternoon. Things were going as planned until all boats returned with the exception of one, by noon anxiety as to its whereabouts had started to grow. Shortly, a change in wind direction ensured that a heavy surf began to break. With the waves beginning to rage many were relieved when, just before 2pm, the boat came into view. However, this relief did not last for long, and it did not take the keenest eye to notice that the boat was having trouble in reaching the shore.

Although a large fishing boat was hauled to the waters edge in an attempt to launch and retrieve the boat's crew, the water proved too troublesome and the attempt was abandoned. Thus, the alarm was raised and the lifeboat was soon manned and pushed out to sea. Whilst facing the waves the lifeboat was nearly overturned, but luckily the boat's buoyancy, an admirable feature, kept the lifeboat afloat. It soon retrieved the men and landed them safely on the beach. Grateful for their lives the crew praised the boat, while the coxswain heavily praised the speed at which the launch was achieved.

Finally after 15 years in service the 'Pelican' retired. The next boat to serve the town was the 'Admiral Rous,' it was provided from the money left by the late Henry John Rous and began its term in service in 1877. The RNLI were given the lifeboat by 'The Victoria Club of London,' a club for ex-servicemen. Although it was smaller than the 'Pelican' it made up for the loss of

Beneath the Guiding Light

space by having a greater width, measuring 30 feet long and 8 feet wide. Unlike the 'Pelican,' the 'Admiral Rous' could be rowed 8 oars single banked. It was 2 years before the lifeboat received its first call spending the first two years of its life unused in the Arthur Street boathouse. However, the boat did not sit idle, being taken out for practice on a regular basis.

The boat was first called out for service on the morning of Thursday 23rd January. It was called to the aid of the Grimsby smack 'Excalibur' and it is a rescue that will never be forgotten. After the alarm had been raised, the lifeboat was rapidly manned and swiftly made its way towards the endangered vessel. Upon approaching the ship, the tide took advantage of its compromising position and tossed the lifeboat against the smack. This vicious attack smashed the oars down one side of the boat, momentarily disabling it. As the crew scrambled to get the reserve oars into position the boat was thrown onto the beach. Yet the action was not over, the crew refused to give up and with the aid of a rope sent via rocket line from the helpless vessel, the lifeboat again approached it's target. By 4pm the struggle was over and the men had been brought safely to shore.

To have the oars break was a common occurrence. When launching the boat it was not unusual for the oars nearest the beach to break as a result of the sea's force, however, a method of prevention was soon devised. During the rescue launch, the lifeboat would be launched up tide from the stranded vessel, then, when the desired position had been reached the crew would drop the anchor and row to the vessel. Thus, by approaching a vessel carefully, the likelihood of breaking the oars was reduced. However, as in the rescue of the 'Excalibur,' it was not uncommon for the oars to be broken on the side of the stranded vessel.

The year of 1883 saw the retirement of the 'Admiral Rous' in which it ended its 6 years of service. During the period between 1877-1883 it made 5 launches and saved 5 lives. Yet just before its retirement in 1881, a new home was under construction for the boat. It was completed in 1882 and can be seen, today, now recognised as the arcade, opposite the Pier Hotel. The new boathouse was constructed at a cost of £375, the money once again coming from the legacy of the late Admiral Henry John Rous. However, the old boathouse was not left uninhabited for long and on the 4th April 1883 it was handed over to the coastguards to house their rocket carts.

Towards the end of 1883 the old 'Admiral Rous' was replaced by another lifeboat at a cost of £363. The money was donated by the Admiral Rous Lifeboat

26

Braving the Sea's Fury

An early lifeboat launch. The cork lifebelts, much different from those of today, are clearly visible.

Beneath the Guiding Light

Fund and thus the boat was named 'Admiral Rous II.' The new boat was larger than the old boat, measuring 34 feet 4inches long and 8 feet 3 inches wide, with 10 oars. Its first call out was received in 1885 although there are no surviving details of this event.

It was during the service of the 'Admiral Rous II' that a great change took place which was to change the fate of the lifeboat service forever. In 1892, work started on the lighthouse and 18 months later in 1894 work had been completed. Upon completion of the lighthouse, the number of call outs the lifeboat service received was drastically cut. For 5 years the 'Admiral Rous II' remained dormant as far as rescues were considered, but this is not to say that the lifeboat remained unused, it still underwent frequent practice sessions as part of the RNLI policy. This policy stated that all boats, whether dormant or in frequent service, should be exercised afloat twice in the summer and twice in the winter, thus ensuring that the lifeboats continued to provide the best service possible.

The 'Admiral Rous II' served the town for a magnificent 28 years. It seems that the boat was preserved due to a comparatively small amount of use, resulting from the navigational aid provided by the lighthouse. However, the lifeboat's term in service was ended in 1911 when a temporary boat, Reserve No 6, the 'Janet Hoyle,' was sent to Withernsea. This was only a temporary arrangement until a new lifeboat could be delivered to the town. It was launched only once during its year long service to the town, this was to the aid of the 'Crux,' a fishing boat that capsized. The dramatic rescue saw the lifeboat make many failed attempts to reach the stranded ship which lay only 100 yards away from the base of the cliff, a situation caused by the force of the tide which was so strong that, despite all efforts, no progress could be made. Yet with the aid of the coastguards the lives of the bruised and battered men were spared and they were returned safely to shore.

The 'Docea Chapman' soon took on the role of the town's lifeboat. During its reign from 1911-1913 it was launched three times and although it was not required to save any lives it did manage to retrieve a vessel. Yet with the ever decreasing number of call outs, greatly reduced by the towns guiding light, the need for a lifeboat was called into question. The newspaper publicly announced the possibility of this on the 24th May 1913, claiming that the crew had been notified that next lifeboat launch may be its last. It also claimed that as a result of the lighthouse "there have been hardly any wrecks in the 20 years that it has cast its warning beam across the sea." Only a week later the 'Docea Chapman' was taken from the

Braving the Sea's Fury

boathouse and transported to Easington. The Withernsea lifeboat was no more.

Although this was intended to be a joyous time, as the lighthouse prevented the unnecessary endangering of lives, the town inhabitants were understandably bitter. To add insult to this all too sudden injury, the locals knew that the lack of a boathouse in Easington resulted in it setting up home under a flimsy canvass. However, the journey of the 'Docea Chapman' is one of great interest. After its move to Easington in 1913 it remained there for 20 years, and afterwards in 1933 it was taken away to take up role in the reserve fleet of lifeboats. However, one year later the lifeboat was returned to service and was sent to Padstow in Cornwall, and this is where it stayed until it was believed that the boat had reached the end of its service. The boat was then bought by the coxswain of the Padstow lifeboat, Tommy Morrissey, who renamed it 'Girl Maureen' and used it as a fishing boat. It was then sold to the Lynmouth Museum, where it is displayed under the name of 'Louisa II,' another praiseworthy lifeboat which had been based at Lynmouth.

However, much to the surprise of the town, in 1974 the lifeboat station reopened. Unlike the early pulling boats, more durable inshore rescue boats now operate throughout the year. Again the crew are volunteers and the lifeboat service is dependent upon donations. Thus the charitable work of Withernsea's first dedicated lifeboat men lives on, accompanied by the great sense of community spirit the lifeboat provides.

Chapter 5

From the Highest Heights
to the Deepest Depths

Churches thrived in Withernsea from a very early age demonstrating the importance of religion in the lives of its inhabitants. The earliest period in which churches may be assumed to have been part of the community is 1115. In this period the Lord of the Seigniory of Holderness, Stephen E. of Albemarle, gave to the Benedictine monk of St Martin de Alceio, near Albemarle in Normandy, some French churches in addition to all of his churches and tythes in England. For the foreign monastery this was a rich windfall inclusive of Paull, Preston, Withernwick, Wawne, Frodingham, Kilnsea and Withernsea, to name but a few. Accordingly, a Prior was sent with a number of monks to take care of the property, although it was not until 1219 when they finally settled down at the chapel of St Helen, in Birstall. It has been recorded that two priests were sent to Withernsea, providing evidence that a church existed in Withernsea from an early era. However the priests didn't survive for long, the rapidly encroaching sea served as a constant worry to the Albemarle Abbots, and in addition to their dislike of the intrusiveness of the civil powers upon their authority, they eventually decided to 'sell out.' So, in the Reign of Richard II, the Holderness possessions were given to the Abbey of Kirstall, in exchange for 10,000 livres.

Shortly after the Abbot's retreat, a second church, the 'Sister Kirke' of St Mary's, was erected in the town. Founded during the reign of King John (1196-1216), the 'Sister Kirke,' or 'Sister Church,' received its name because of the adjacent church built simultaneously in the village of Owthorne. Tradition holds that the adjoining manors were in the possession of two sisters, both of whom wanted to provide a place of worship not only for themselves but also for their tenants. While the church underwent construction, a quarrel broke out between the women who found it impossible to decide whether it should have a tower or a spire. The argument continued and eventually the sisters agreed to disagree, resulting in each building a church of their own. The church at Owthorne was named St Peter's, whilst the one at Withernsea was named St Mary's, hence the churches became known as the 'Sister Churches.'

In days when religion touched the life of almost everyone, it comes as no surprise to discover that the villagers of Hollym were dependant upon the church of Withernsea and thus the 'Sister Church' of St Mary's was not, as intended, only used for the inhabitants of the small village of Withernsea.

From the Highest Heights to the Deepest Depths

Permission for its own church was granted to the village in 1409, partly due to the growing fear of overcrowding in the Withernsea church, to which the inhabitants of Hollym were parishioners.

But gradually, the sea encroached upon the 'Sister Church' of Withernsea, washing away its churchyard in the early 15th Century. By 1444, the church lay at complete mercy to the waves and it wasn't long before it was totally demolished, leaving the town's inhabitants without a place of worship. Shortly afterwards a meeting was held and it was decided that another church should be built in a less vulnerable position, thus Priests Hill was chosen as the site for the new church. Plans were drawn and by 1488 the church was completed and dedicated to St Nicholas. Consisting of a chancel with vestry, nave with aisles and a tower at the western end, the church stood as one of the most architecturally detailed constructions that the villagers had ever seen. The internally oak chancel roof was supported via five pairs of brackets decorated with carved sculptures of angels and shields which looked down upon the parishioners. The nave roof consisted of a similar construction which also rested upon brackets. Accessible by two entrances, the church was entered by a porch on the southern side and a door on the northern part. In addition to this the northern part of St Nicholas was built of cobblestones retrieved from the beach, it had ashlar-cornered buttresses and battlements. In the tower stood a pillar of Saxon character, it is presumed that this was retrieved from the old edifice which had disappeared in 1444. However, the arch of the chancel and the arch which protrudes from the east wall of the nave rest upon brackets which appear to be of an earlier date that 1444. The two chancel brackets represent angels with black shields and the two nave brackets are a monsters head and angel with a shield, the latter of which are the earlier.

The church stood tall and proud until 1609, when a great storm raged along the coastline destroying the roof of the church. However, the villagers continued to use the church until the early 17th Century, when it became completely unusable. When this happened a role reversal took place and the Hollym chapel served the whole parish. It is presumed that the 'Sister Church' at Owthorne, St Peter's, still stood but was rendered too small for both populations.

Despite the apparent God fearing attitude of the local inhabitants, religion was not always capable of deterring people from sin. One scandalous tale has come to light, concerning Adam Alvin, a man fearless in the face of God. This anonymous newspaper extract is believed to originate from around the mid-18th Century:

Beneath the Guiding Light

Murder at Owthorne:
"During the early 1690's a young woman was washed up on the beach at Owthorne from the wreck of a ship. She was clutching a young baby in her arms, and both mother and child suffering badly from the cold, were taken to the vicarage where the mother died shortly afterwards. However, the baby survived and after much advertising the child still was not claimed. It was finally decided that the child should stay at the vicarage, not as the vicar's son, but as a potential workman around the house and grounds. Aware that his position was a lowly one, the young lad grew up to be a morose and sullen youth who was unpopular in the village.

The vicar's house consisted of himself, Reverend Henock Sinclair, his two nieces, Mary and Catherine Sinclair, and the now grown up Adam Alvin. In spite of his surly character, Adam managed to gain the affections of Mary - much to the annoyance of the vicar who angrily forbad this liaison. The solution to this problem was that Adam must get rid of the vicar, he proceeded to do this presumably with the full knowledge and even support of the two nieces.

In early June 1708, Alvin murdered Henock Sinclair and buried his body in the vicarage garden. He then saddled and bridled the vicar's horse and left it some miles from the village. The report was then circulated that the vicar had set off on a journey the previous day and had disappeared, probably over the cliffs, as his hat and wig were found on the beach. The villagers were suspicious and soon ugly rumours had spread associating Adam's name with the vicar's disappearance. Yet nothing could be proved against him, especially as the nieces had supported his story.

Within two months, on the 29th August 1708, Adam and Mary were secretly married at Halsham on a special licence. The people at Owthorne were outraged when they learnt of this, and shortly afterwards the three conspirators left the district and moved to London.

Four years later, Catherine Sinclair suffered a serious illness, and to ease her conscience, it is understood that she made a full confession of her part in the crime and indicated where the body could be found. Alvin and his wife were soon arrested in London and set on trial in York. Alvin was convicted and his wife was acquitted.

During the preaching of the condemned sermon, Alvin loudly proclaimed his innocence, this so offended the preacher, the Reverend Mr Mace, that he had a seizure and fell down dead. "See" said Alvin, "the hand of God visibly

From the Highest Heights to the Deepest Depths

The Church of St Nicholas in its early days

33

Beneath the Guiding Light

displayed." However, when faced with death the following morning, he fully confessed to the crime and was duly hanged.

Did Adam murder, or kill the vicar by accident during one of the many outbursts of his uncontrollable temper? Many believed the latter until an early entry in the Owthorne Overseers Book of the 4th May 1708, unearthed the mystery. The vicar possessed a property of the annual value of £12. The year after the murder the vicar's name drops out and Alvin's name appears. So it seems that it was nothing more than a devious plot."

Despite the rapid erosion of the clay cliffs which had already claimed the medieval church of St Mary's, the Owthorne church of St Peter's still stood. However, it was replaced in 1801 by a new church surprisingly named St Mary's, this can now be located in the village of Rimswell. Unfortunately, although outliving it's corresponding 'Sister Church,' it wasn't long before St Peter's lay at the mercy of the tides, by 1816 its graveyard had started to erode leaving corpses littering the beach and peering hauntingly from the cliff face. A huge task lay ahead, not entirely the most elegant job, the grim task of leading the bones to Rimswell for reburial took a total of 15 days. However, the approaching sea was not the only threat posed to the corpses, a different concern for the dead is illustrated by this account from the Hull and Yorkshire Times:

"One night Mr Jackson and his wife were standing outside their cottage when they discerned in the moonlight a number of figures moving about in the site of the old church and on the shore beneath. They were body snatchers who had journeyed up from London to secure in easy fashion, material for their eerie trade. A grim relic of their visit was found by Mr Jackson when he visited the cliff top during the next day. It was a crowbar, and it had apparently been used to prise open the coffins that had withstood the onslaught of the sea. Not long after this incident coastguards were sent to watch over the site of the old church and the eerie visitations were stopped."

The new church built at Rimswell, was for many residents of Owthorne, too far out, and thus in 1850 work started on a the chapel of St Matthews, which was built in Waxholme Road, now Queen Street, resolving the problem. It is believed that one vicar served both places which resulted in a Rectory being built on Hull Road, as it was the central place between the two. This temporary arrangement was continued for over 80 years until the new Owthorne church, St Matthew's, was built on Hull Road in 1935. Gradually, the two towns merged into one and Withernsea became known as the town

34

From the Highest Heights to the Deepest Depths

with two churches. When this happened, St Mary's church at Rimswell became accepted as the villages own church.

With the divergence of religion in the 19th Century, Withernsea saw a rapid increase in the number of churches located within the town. Wesleyan Methodism emerged and in 1809 and to support its few founding members, a tiny chapel was built in Barb Lane, now known as North Gate. As membership increased a second Wesleyan chapel was erected in Cammidge Street in 1858. However, by the 20th Century the congregation had outgrown the second chapel and in 1901 the Wesleyan's third church opened in Queen Street, a time during which the second chapel was demolished. With its fine architecture and high steeple, it was one of the few impressive buildings in Withernsea. Ironically, this grand building was constructed by W. N. Carr, the chapel steward of the Primitive Methodists, opposers of the Wesleyans.

The Primitive Methodists founded their first chapel in the village of Tunstall in 1812. The rapidly spreading cult soon reached Withernsea, and in 1848 the Withernsea Primitive Methodists Society formed with three original members. Although initially they couldn't afford a chapel, they were not put off, and met for prayer meetings and occasional services in retrospective houses, by 1858 they had the funds they needed and built a chapel in Alma Street. In 1879, when membership had increased, they opened their second chapel in Hull Road, which still exists and is in active use today.

Although the two forms of Methodism were in constant competition, by 1902 they had learnt to work in harmony. They agreed to a union in 1932, a movement that was taken slowly due to resistance, but was completed by the 1960's. The architecturally exquisite Wesleyan chapel situated on Queen Street served as a meeting place until, due to an unsound structure, it was demolished in 1976, and from that date the chapel on Hull Road was the one used for worship. Wesley Court, a block of sheltered accommodation for the elderly, was built on the old site of the Wesleyan chapel.

Another great change that occurred in the 19th Century was the rebuilding of the St Nicholas church, which after losing its roof, remained in a state of ruin for 250 years. It was only when the railway arrived that the town's prosperity increased to such an extent that it was able to consider building a new church. In 1855, when the Archbishop of York visited the site he decided that the once beautiful construction should not be allowed to go to waste, and hence the decision was made to rebuild the old church. Meanwhile, the Archbishop performed weekly services in the Station waiting room,

Beneath the Guiding Light

subscription to which went towards the cost of rebuilding the church. Money was also generously donated by the 'Hull and Holderness Railway Company,' as well as raised by a book about churches written by the Reverend A. Gatty, vicar of Ecclesfield. The vicar's interest in this project was aroused whilst on holiday in the town in 1850. Thus in the year of 1859 the church was rebuilt, Cuthbert Brodrick did the work, building the new St Nicholas church around the derelict carcass of the old one at a cost of £12,000. It was rebuilt chiefly of beach cobblestones, and quarried stone was used for the chancel, buttresses and battlements. The old bells had been lost and were therefore replaced by a single bell in the western tower. There are now seven bells in the church, the last of which was donated in 1948. Withernsea is constantly indebted to these ambitious entrepreneurs for their initiative, as without them, St Nicholas would probably have remained derelict for many more years and perhaps may never have been restored.

However, the 19th Century not only witnessed the celebratory renewal of this important church, but also unearthed many sad memories from the past. A newspaper extract dated 21st August 1897 claims:

"Whilst excavating an old drain on the old farm premises being demolished at South Cliff, Mr Found's workmen discovered a large quantity of Derbyshire stone, apparently belonging to some ecclesiastical building. The fragments, which consisted chiefly of the mullions of a window, had been used to form the top of a drain, and had been ruthlessly cut and chipped to fit the shape of the drain, which appears to have gone round the building. A millstone, not very much used, was also excavated with the other. In all probability the mullions are relics of the old church of Owthorne, which was dismantled by a storm in 1796. In 1816, a large portion of the eastern end of the church fell, and was washed down the cliff, and in 1822 Poulson states that the chancel, nave, and part of the tower were gone and in 1838 scarcely any remnant of the churchyard was left. It is hardly probable that the stone would be taken from St Nicholas' church now called, which from 1609-1859 was in a state of ruin, although not impossible. The large quantity, however, suggests that it was carted from the beach when part of the old church fell, and the presence of the mill stone lends a little colour to this supposition as a mill stood adjacent to the church. It is also stated that the owner of the land on which the farm stood at that time, exercised the rights of the lord of the manor and claimed the wreckage on the beach."

This was not the only part of the old Owthorne church of St Peter's to be reclaimed, as an interesting letter published in the Eastern Morning News on

From the Highest Heights to the Deepest Depths

Tuesday 4th August 1896 displays:

Owthorne Font:
"Mr Harwood Brierlay in his interesting East Yorkshire itinerary (No.XX) says - "What became of the ancient Owthorne font, I have not heard say." In a little front garden in Leicester Street, Hull, there is a font, in a good state of preservation, which Alderman J. Symons, Hull, says is the Owthorne font. I well remember, when living in Leicester Street, Alderman Symons and the late G. Lancaster paying me a visit, and among other things the worthy Alderman told me he had been paying a visit to the Owthorne font in the garden nearly opposite; that he hastened to buy it, but the people would not part with it, and asked me to keep an eye on it. This I do. Some of our older fonts have done duty as horse troughs; others as ornaments in rockeries; this one is a flower stand. The former clock bells of the Driffield Linseed Cake Mill were said to be made out of Owthorne church bells, and when the mill was burnt down some years ago the melted bell metal was purchased by Messrs. Shipham, brass founders, Hull, and much of it made into hand bells, gongs, and ash trays, which were presented to friends. I possess one of the ash trays, and a beautiful sound it gives out when struck."
(J. Nicholson, Hull).

Thus, as the 19th Century drew to a close, with the renovation of St Nicholas and the reminder of churches long gone, it appeared that the town had dedicated enough land to places of worship. However, this was not the case and the turn of the century, the year of 1903, saw the Congregational church established on the corner of Lee Avenue. 1972 saw the Congregational church unite with the Presbyterian church of England, and emerge renamed as the United Reformed church which still plays an active role in the community today.

After the emancipation of Catholic faith in 1892, Catholic churches established themselves throughout the kingdom. As there were few Catholics in Withernsea they had to travel to Hull or Hedon for Sunday mass. Eventually, after much debate, a tiny wooden church was built and when the Marist Fathers came to Hull, they took responsibility for the Catholics of Withernsea. It was a happy day for many when in May 1936 Withernsea was established as a parish and a new church was built in Bannister Street, dedicated to St Peter and St John Fisher. To this day services continue to be held in the small, but beautiful, church.

The importance of religion is demonstrated by the role it plays in the lives of many people today. Although the churches of the town have held a long

Beneath the Guiding Light

and varied reign in the town, they continue to play a prominent role in society, exhibiting how time not only brings about change, but also a reassuring sense of stability which evolves from a longstanding tradition, which has succeeded in a world of endless confusion.

Chapter 6

The Legend of Will O' Withernsea

The 2000th edition of the Gazette, issued on the 20th June 1969, contained a story, sent to the Editor by a German correspondent. It appears that the story of Will O' Withernsea has been a longstanding German folktale, much to the town's surprise. The tale is set in the early days of Withernsea, when the town was nothing more than a small collection of white painted cobbled huts set within close proximity to the sea. The inhabitants of the town during this period made their living by fishing and by salvaging goods from the many wreckages that fell prey to the stormy coastline. The tale claims that a young girl from the town took up employment with a Hull merchant shipping family, assuming the position of the family's maid. Hull, during this period, was a bustling port and thus had many temporary visitors from far and wide. Within a short time, as is often the case in folktales, the sheltered young maid succumbed to the temptation of the port and fell in love with a handsome sailor, whose history although rather elusive, is believed to have a "visage swarthy as the ripe blackberry and he was accounted of foreigne parts." Hence, it became generally accepted that the sailor was a Spaniard.

Unluckily, after this encounter the girl fell pregnant. Shamed into giving up her job, she returned to the small hamlet of Withernsea where nine months later she gave birth to a son who she named Will. Unlike the villagers who, as tradition held, had the fair complexion of the Danes, the young baby was as dark as his father, a trait which led to instant rejection by the villagers. This matter was not helped by the fact that the child was disfigured and sported a humped back, which the superstitious villagers claimed to be the girls punishment by God.

Despite his seemingly cursed appearance, Will grew up a happy child, not thinking of himself as any different from any of the other children he had come across. His kind nature ensured that he was always ready to lend a hand whenever required, expecting nothing in return. However, by the age of 8 a gap began to form between Will and the other village children, whereas the other young boys went to sea with their fathers, Will, the illegitimate child, could not. None of the seamen would allow him on board their boats believing that this mysterious child seemed to have the ability to see into the future and would serve only to curse their journey. At first many of the villagers had believed that Will's ability to find things was simply because his dark eyes were sharper than their blue ones, they often heard tales of how marvellous he was at helping his grandmother find her wool 'Tek a peep 'neath your chair, Granny. The cat took it there yestermorn.' Much to her astonishment it

Beneath the Guiding Light

was there. Yet this ability to see into the future developed with age and as Will grew older he began to share his gift. On many occasions he had warned sailors not to go to sea for fear of a storm, but when they glanced up at the blue, cloudless skies they put his warnings down to jealousy and scorned his behaviour. However, when the waves began to swell they soon realised that Will's warnings were right. Despite his many accurate predictions, instead of trusting Will, the villagers began to fear him, and, believing that he had the ability to curse people, it wasn't long before they wouldn't let him within 50 yards of their boats.

As Will matured, his lack of experience at sea, forced him to become a cobbler. His career was successful and even though "his shoen and bootes were much regarded as the beste on the whole coaste," Will was unhappy. He would often spend hours enviously looking out towards sea longing to be a sailor like all the other villagers. The women who passed by, upon seeing his tears believed that he was crying for a wife, but no one would take him because of his unsightly appearance.

However, one night when the fishermen gathered for a drink, Will ran amongst them and cried "Lads, its going to come soon, I tell yer!" When asked what he was ranting on about he replied "The big flood." He continued by telling them that Withernsea would be swallowed up by the waves, but all was not lost, he told them "Will will save thee. Touch me hump just once and tha'll be all right... where there's a Will there's a way." After this bizarre outburst many of the villagers became too scared to travel out to sea, but soon they were struck with the reality that a huge wave could sweep away the village at any time, so their fear turned to anger. Will, seeing that no one would take caution, continued to warn the villagers. However, anger increased and they threatened to send him to the magistrates at Beverley on the grounds that he was a wizard, if he continued with these ludicrous tales.

Yet all was not lost and he claimed the belief of one villager. A pretty young maid only 16 years old believed in Will's claim that "Where there's a Will there's a way" and touched his hump. Unbeknown to her, she was to be the only one saved when the flood arrived.

On the 2nd December 1678 a storm began to rage, striking boats as far as 8 miles off Withernsea. However, being men well adapted to ferocious seas, the sailors were not afraid, almost excited by the challenge that lay ahead. However, these fearless men were soon in a helpless situation when their boats were swamped by the raging waves. Despite the crews attempt to put up

The Legend of Will O' Withernsea

Fishing has always been part of the local heritage, although fewer livelihoods depend on it now than in days gone by.

Beneath the Guiding Light

a brave fight, the hungry waves rapidly devoured them. Not satisfied with it's triumph, the stirring waves soon began to pound against the low, sandy cliffs upon which the small hamlet of Withernsea was perched. The cliff put up little resistance, and soon the waves were pounding against the sides of the cottages. Fear welled within the villagers as they realised that there was no escape and they wished that they had listened to Will. But it was too late and soon the windows gave in, leaving the villagers to accept their merciless fate as they were swept out to sea. It is believed that on that night 43 boats were sunk or wrecked.

When dawn broke Will and the young maid awoke to find that the old Withernsea had vanished and it seemed that Will's words were true when he said that "Where there's a Will there's a way." It is believed that the house where the two survivors lived was situated upon the grounds where the Alma Hotel is now located, part of the cobbled stone wall, claimed to be the remains of the house, still exists serving as longstanding evidence of the truth behind this tale.

Chapter 7

It's Time to Learn

There was no primary school system in England in the year 1800, but this was soon to change. Previously, the only education children had been able to receive was provided by the sparse religious charity schools and the local dame schools, in this period the state accepted no responsibility for educational matters. However, the early 19th Century saw efforts being made to make education more widely available to the masses.

With the slowly increasing populations of Hollym and Withernsea, rising, in 1823, to approximately 203 and 103, respectively, it came as no surprise that a school was opened in Withernsea to support the education of the village's children. With the attendance of 20 boys and 15 girls, the children were educated at their parents expense. Due to its tiny population it soon became more conventional for Withernsea children to attend the recently opened schools in Owthorne and Hollym and shortly afterwards the main school of the growing town, the Owthorne National School, was up and running. On inspection day in 1871, there were 38 boys in attendance, and two private schools in the area were attended by 42 girls and 4 boys.

Before the 1870's the schools in Withernsea were small, private ventures, the survival of which was dependent upon the fees paid by parents and offerings from religious subscribers. But by the 1870's these schools were insufficient and simply could not cater for the needs of all the children in the area. This was the general feeling for the country as a whole. It was estimated that by 1867 one and a half million children were in attendance of the voluntary, mainly church schools, and that approximately two and a half million should be attending, but were not.

In response to this W. E. Forsters Education Act of 1870 introduced state provided and state maintained elementary schools out of public funds. This revolutionary act was to change the face of education forever. It stated that schools were to be provided and run by School Boards, which should be elected by the ratepayers of the area on a three yearly basis. A scheme was set up whereby the board met their expenses by fees and government grants, and it was generally agreed that if a deficit occurred they were able to demand that the remainder was paid by the ratepayers. The power to control expenditure was given to the Board, but, to avoid overspending, the accounts had to be checked regularly by the District Auditor.

Thus in accordance with the Act, the Owthorne Board School was erected on Hull Road. At a cost of £2,000, it aimed to educate the children of the

Beneath the Guiding Light

rapidly expanding district of Owthorne and Withernsea. The average attendance in the year of 1878-79 was 95. The school building was extremely small in comparison to the schools of today, comprising only one large classroom, a board room and the head's room. The building, although small, was capable of providing 150 places, although in the year of 1878 only 103 children were enrolled, mainly due to the fact that attendance was not made compulsory until 1880.

As the years passed by it became increasingly evident that this seemingly infallible system was seriously flawed, and in September of 1883 it was recorded in the School Board Minutes that a total deficit of £17.14s had arisen which would have to be raised by the townships. Thus it was decided that, both in the interests of the ratepayers as well as the headmaster, the size of the government grant needed to be increased. For this to be made financially viable the education system required a makeover. So, it was decided upon that the main focal point was to be upon the performance of the children in their annual examination. In an attempt to attain this target, the methods of education were totally reorganised. The work for each year was set out in the Department of Education code and each year's work was put to external scrutiny by the Department Inspectors. Hence, the annual examination dominated the whole educational year, not only did it determine the work given to the children, but upon the results depended the amount of money offered to the school.

Government grants were not the only source of income for schools, they were also dependent upon school fees. At the Board meeting in March 1878, the fees were fixed at the following amounts:
Infants (5-7 yrs): 3d per week.
Above 7: 6d per week.
Two or more infants: 2d each, and 4d for over 7's
The Act stipulated that no family should pay more than 9d per week.

This money was payable in advance on Monday mornings, yet many families were unwilling to pay these fees and fell into arrears. A campaign in which the Board stated how they would deal with this problem was up and running by 1881. To begin with a letter would be sent to the parents, if this failed they would be summoned before the board, and finally, if all else failed they would be summoned before a magistrate. This campaign was continued until 1891 when a new Education Act abolished school fees and provided an extra government grant to make up the deficit. This system only applied to elementary education, as secondary education, in the 19th Century, was still

It's Time to Learn

only available to those people who could afford the fees for public or endowed grammar schools.

However, with compulsory and free education for those below the age of 12, the school soon became unable to facilitate the local children. From the start many had said that the school, originally intended to house 150, simply wasn't big enough to accommodate the children from the surrounding area. In 1891 it had 140 pupils and by the summer of 1893 the total had risen to 210. It was at this point that extra rooms were built by John Wilkinson at a cost of £595. By the turn of the Century the school had five members of staff and an astounding 265 children!

School Boards were abolished in 1902 by an important Act of Parliament, which, in turn brought Board Schools under total control of the Local Education Authority. The Owthorne District Board School became the Withernsea Council School and by 1903 it also contained a separate infants department. A temporary building for the infants was supplied in 1905, it was a green, corrugated iron hut and cost £150. A major improvement occurred in 1906 when this was replaced by a new block and the main building was further enlarged to provide a new department. These new buildings ensured that all 224 pupils were adequately housed. The pupils aged 7-14 were situated in the building near the road, whilst the infants were placed in the building behind the playground.

These buildings were put to full use by 1908, when the school was thriving. Not only was the educational standard higher than it had ever been before, but the school was also in excellent order and capable of providing its students with a quality education without the added stress of overcrowding, although the classes were still large by today's standards. Mr Edward Downes, for example, had a class of 85 children, which were of course kept in order by the harsh disciplinary rules of the early 20th Century.

It didn't take long to realise that this extra room was not sufficient, with the population of the town continuously rising it was decided that more building work was required. The next phase of construction took place between 1913 and 1915 in which the main building was extended, although the infants block had been slightly enlarged in 1909. This extension consisted of a new assembly hall, cookery room and teachers restroom, two new classrooms were also erected. In addition to this the building also received improved cloakroom facilities, as well as a shelter in the enlarged playground. By this time there were 287 pupils.

Beneath the Guiding Light

The attendance figures continued to rise at an astounding pace, rising from 272 in 1906 to 424 in 1918. Again accommodation was beginning to become problematical, and by 1920 it had become so acute that it was impossible for the infants to be sent to the junior department, as was the previous arrangement, due to a sheer lack of space. In an attempt to solve this problem the Board Managers tried to secure some land at the South end of Withernsea for the prospect of future school extensions, but this came to nothing. Luckily, plans for the suggested Withernsea Central School were passed in 1920, and by 1921 the school had become so crowded that the top two classes had to be held in the hall, a class at each end. Thus the school had become divided into separate senior and junior departments. Due to overcrowding, the official opening of the Withernsea Central School, which was to take place on the 5th September 1921, was too far away to wait until and so pupils occupied it from June 1921, leaving the infants and juniors to use the old school.

Yet, this 'new' building was not what would be considered a suitable school today. It consisted of two ex army wooden huts which represented an 'E' shape, an open veranda was situated on the eastern side. Three teachers were sent there with two classes and thus Miss Scott was left in charge of the rest of the school, the title of which had changed from 'Withernsea County School - Mixed Department' to 'Withernsea Junior School.' The attendance of both schools continued to rise significantly and by 1922 the attendance of the Senior School, now the Junior School, was 126, whilst the Junior School had 402 students. This had increased to 273 and 362 respectively by 1935.

The old school huts, however, brought in floods of complaints and were the subject of many heated arguments between the Withernsea Council and the local LEA at County Hall, Beverley. Managers put their foot down about the huts in 1930 and insisted that "the time had now arrived when a permanent school should be erected." Eventually, after much debate, they were replaced but unfortunately, due to the national financial situation, the building could not be completed until 1934. At a cost of £11,000, it was built by the Doncaster firm of T. Jenkinson and Sons Ltd. Initially the school consisted of four classrooms along each wing, with both a science laboratory and administration rooms which were positioned centrally.

Careful plans were made for the opening ceremony of the school. The children would walk in procession from the hall of the Junior School to the new school, where the county architect would present the key to the 'opener,' Lord Halifax. Afterwards, everyone would assemble in the new hall, where

It's Time to Learn

the school choir would lead the hymn 'These Things Shall Be,' followed by prayers by a minister of the church. Finally, speeches would follow and the proceedings would be completed by 'Jerusalem' and 'The National Anthem.' Light refreshments would then be served in the old Junior School.

During the outbreak of war in 1939 the school remained open, many evacuees were boarded in Withernsea which resulted in the school roll rising to just above 400, comprising 260 Withernsea children and 140 evacuees. The evacuees were accompanied by four members of staff from Hull but arrangements had to be made to provide accommodation for them. Tables borrowed from the Primitive Methodist Chapel and the Wesleyan Chapel ensured that three classes, for a while, could be accommodated in the hall. September of 1940 saw some of the Hull teachers return to the city and the remaining children were merged into normal classes. By this time the classes were once again very crowded, but the worst was still to come.

In August of 1942, Miss Longdon's log book reported that bombs had been released near the lighthouse and machine gun fire had sprayed Hull road, but no real damage had been caused and thankfully the schools had not been targeted. However, on the 13th June 1943, the book reports that "incendiary bombs fell on the department. Classroom 8 was completely burnt out. There is a hole in the hall and on the platform." In this state of urgency, and luckily without any injuries, some classes had to be accommodated in the Methodist Chapel. This arrangement was continued for the full school year until the damage could be repaired and the classroom was in a satisfactory state of repair.

In 1944, after the disturbance of the bomb scare, the Education Act decided upon the reshaping of the stages of school education. Schools for children below the age of 11 became 'primary' instead of 'elementary,' and those for children above that age became 'secondary.' There were no fees to be paid in state schools and the day started with an act of worship, compulsory to all. By 1948 the school leaving age had been raised to 15. To cater for the raising of the school leaving age the HORSA huts were built, named after the 'Organisation of Huts for the Raising of the School leaving Age programme.' In addition to this the school became bilateral with grammar school and secondary modern sides, and was thus a forerunner of the comprehensive system. Again the school expanded its reach taking, in addition to all the local children aged 11 and above, children from villages as far away as Hedon, Preston and Paull. In 1948 the name officially changed to Withernsea High School. However, by 1950 further accommodation problems had arisen

Beneath the Guiding Light

resulting in an extra classroom being added to each wing of the school, the west one was to serve as a library.

Due to lack of space, a new High School building was opened in 1955. The juniors moved into the old High School and the infants into the old Junior School, to form the complex seen today. The High School underwent further expansion in 1963 and 1971 and various additions were later made. By 1980 the number of pupils on the roll for each of the schools was charted at 1,350 for the High School, the junior School had 370 in attendance, whilst the Infant School had 230 pupils

Today the High School still thrives on the success that it has always had, now supporting an Adult Education centre and serving as a 6th form college. Whether the scholars be young or old the school still upholds the same standards which Mr Shaw rigidly believed in:

"Every pupil deserved to be given the opportunity of developing his gifts (wherever they may lay) to the full. No arbitrary limit was to be placed on his possible achievement. We never tried to say "you are not capable of that," and we were often astonished at the outcome."

(W. H. Shaw - ex Headmaster - 1956-1974).

Chapter 8

Fame at Last

Over the years the town has harboured a silent pride, watching as its children have risen to fame, shining in all their glory and astounding the world. Many people remain in ignorance of the stars who have been born or even dwelt in the town, and many are unaware of the best selling novel based upon Withernsea. Nevertheless, the town continues to cling to its secrets. One of its most famous ex-residents is Kay Kendall, a local girl who hit Hollywood fame in the 1950's. She became a household name both in England and the United States and co-starred with many famous actors including Gene Kelly and Yul Brynner.

Kay was born in Stanley House, a home that still retains its name and can be found along Hull Road. With an older brother and sister, Terry and Kim, Kay was one of three children born to the Kendall's. Performing was in the bloodstream, Kay's mother, Gladys Drewery (believed to be a collateral descendant of Captain Cook), and her father, Terence Kendall, were both stage dancers. Terence's mother, Marie Kendall, was also a famous stage performer who was considered, by Edwardian society, to be the 'darling' of the music hall. Ultimately, Kay followed in the footsteps of her ancestors and studied ballet for six years with the Russian ballerina Lydia Kyash.

When the Second World War began, Kay, then 12, and her family were evacuated to London. It was at this point that she began her career by touring in stage shows as part of the chorus line, she even made an appearance in the London Palladium with her sister, Kim. It was this determination that caused Kay's talent to shine and everyone believed that she was well on her way to success. Later fully fledged in independence Kay's mother, Gladys, suggested that she perform a double act with her sister, and they began to produce shows to entertain the American troops. However, this was brought to an end when, at the age of 18, Kim was called up for service and Kay, now only 17, was chosen to play a showgirl in a film called 'London Town.' Eventually, to her astonishment, she was given the leading role, but sadly for Kay the film was a million pound flop. Kay's disappointment was obvious when she recalled "London Town was such a disaster I left the country for 2 years and went round with touring repertory companies in Germany and Italy learning how to act." At this point Kay was under contract to J. Arthur Rank, her ego had been badly bruised and Kay's determination began to rapidly diminish.

When the war ended, Kay spent much of her time modelling for glamour magazines, until she found the break she was looking for when she was cast

49

Beneath the Guiding Light

with Kenneth More in the 1953 film 'Genevieve,' a tale of two friendly rivals in the London to Brighton vintage car race. You can imagine Kay's delight when the film was acclaimed one of Britain's biggest commercial hits and was given an Academy Award. 'Genevieve' had launched Kay into stardom and she was now known as the girl having "more allure in her eyes than

Kay Kendall (right) with her sister, Kim (left).

Fame at Last

Marilyn Monroe has from top to toe" (Picturegoer, 1954). Almost overnight Kay had become the 'it girl,' she was a trendsetter, and was in great demand as a model. Meanwhile, the British producers reproached themselves for having ignored her for so long! After this initial success Kay was in high demand, she starred in many films, her most popular being; 'The Constant Husband' in 1954, 'Simon and Laura' in 1955, 'Les girls' in 1957, 'The Reluctant Debutante' in 1958 and 'Once More With Feeling' in 1958.

Kay was married to Rex Harrison, the star of 'My Fair Lady' and 'Dr Doolittle,' in an after midnight ceremony which took place in New York on 23rd June 1957. Yet, not being one to boast, she had a second ceremony especially for close friends and family a week later in a friends garden. Kay, the down to earth girl that she was, didn't make a great show about the wedding. As Kay's sister, Kim, recalls, "She and Rex were so happy and giggling so much that the minister had to halt proceedings and say, 'Miss Kendall, unless you can take this more seriously, I shall be unable to continue'." But this showed Kay as she really was, not an egotistical star, but as a happy soul with a desire to appreciate every moment of life.

Kay was delighted when she and her husband, Rex, shared the screen together in Vincent Minelli's production of 'The Reluctant Debutante' in 1958. Both on screen and off Kay and Rex shone as the team they undoubtedly were. Even Kay claimed "The Reluctant Debutant was the nicest thing to happen following our marriage...Most important was the fact that we worked together as husband and wife in the film." Yet this blissful period was not to last forever, and it was during this year that Kay began to show signs of illness.

Thus, in 1958 came the film, which, as the title suggested, was to be her last. In 'Once More With Feeling' Kay starred alongside Yul Brynner but filming was temporarily interrupted when she became ill. The determination that singled Kay from other performers as a child again took over and with a struggle the film was eventually finished, but sadly, Kay died of Leukaemia a year later on the 11th September 1959, at a youthful age of 32. Her roller coaster career had already spanned an amazing 22 years, during which she had travelled the world as a film star, and made around 30 films. Her death struck a chord with many, even the critics could not hide their emotion, claiming, "Kay Kendall was superb in 'Once More With Feeling,' her death a year later stole a possible all-time great from the screens of the future." (Picturegoer). It was clear that this view was held by all, and Kay's memory lives on in the display at the Lighthouse Museum in Withernsea, which was

Beneath the Guiding Light

Kay in her teenage years.

Fame at Last

set up and lovingly dedicated to her by her sister Kim, as a monument for all to behold.

Even before the world was graced with Kay's existence, the town witnessed the birth of another star to be, Kenny Baker, the world renowned trumpet player. After the First World War had achieved a sense of closure, Kenny's father and mother, both shoemakers, decided to set up their business in the rapidly growing town of Withernsea. His mother, a talented musician, taught music and dancing in the town, often putting on shows in the Floral Hall. In 1921 Kenny was born at 73 Queen Street, unknown to his family, their son's life was going to be one fruited with success.

Kenny's love and talent for music had shown itself from a youthful age. By the age of 13, and with a little encouragement from his mother, he had already started to play the coronet in the Gospel Mission Band. He also played the trumpet in the town's band, and was not put off by the formality of the public appearances where they dressed in smart blue uniforms to perform to the demanding crowds. Little did they know that the entrepreneur musician was later to become Britain's leading trumpeter, starring alongside some of the nation's greatest stars.

In the 1930's the family moved to Hull. Kenny's love of music stayed with him and he joined the West Silver Prize Excelsior Band where he continued to play until 1939, after which he moved back to the Midlands. Later Kenny joined the Lew Stone orchestra and, due to his growing reputation, was soon in great demand among the star orchestras of the time. During this period he worked with many great bands such as Ambrose, Jack Jackson, Jack Hylton and Geraldo. Kenny was slowly rising to fame and soon began to make his mark on the London Jazz scene with people like George Shearing, George Chisholm, Harry Parry and many others. He was also frequently played on the radio and setting recording dates.

The war halted his growing reputation, just as it put an end to the orderly lives of the British citizens, and Kenny was forced to join the RAF in 1942. During these 5 years of his life his love for music continued to shine, leading to occasional work with the 'Squadronaires', as well as programmes opposite the Glen Miller Band.

In 1946 Baker's fame continued to escalate and he went on to become the lead trumpet of the Ted Heath Band, one of his best known compositions of this period is 'Bakerloo - non-stop.' The band also performed music for

Beneath the Guiding Light

'London Town,' a film featuring Kay Kendall, although Kenny was unaware that he and the glamorous star shared the same hometown. After 3 years he left the band and formed his own band, which included performers such as Tubby Hayes and Stan Tracey. His career during this period also included top billings with such names as Morecambe and Wise, Ken Dodd, Jimmy James, Tommy Trinder and Benny Hill. In addition to this he worked in the film industry with people like Robert Fornan and Stanley Black. Kenny once again encountered Kay when he went to do a recording for a film which was tipped to be a huge hit. The music was to be used in the film 'Genevieve' and was to be mimed to by Kay, ironically both were still ignorant of the other's birthplace.

In 1952, Kenny was asked by the BBC producer, Pat Dixon, to front a group which was to be called 'Bakers Dozen.' In a short time, this developed into a highly successful radio programme which spanned 7 years called 'Lets Settle For Music.' After another spell in variety, and a great deal of touring, Baker decided to stay in London where he could return to studio work. This line of work brought him into contact with a vast range of stars, Michael Bentine (Square World), Spike Milligan (The Goons), Laurie Johnson (The Avengers), John Barrie (James Bond) and The Beatles. His work was filled with variety, ranging from symphony to Top of the Pops. Shortly afterwards Baker joined the Jack Parnell Orchestra at ATV Studio's in Elstree, where, once again, he brushed shoulders with stars such as Tom Jones, Engelbert Humperdink, Barbara Streisland, Burt Bacharach, and, perhaps most famously, the cast of the Muppet Show. Other people he has worked with include Bing Crosby, Frank Sinatra, Tony Bennet, Sammy Davis, Lena Horne, Peggy Lee, Benny Goodman and Bill May, to name but a few.

The year of 1984 saw the British Academy of Songwriters, Composers and Authors award the Gold Badge of Merit to Kenny. Previously he had won the Melody Maker poll for the Best Jazz Musician in 1942 and afterwards continued to top the polls for many years. He also won the British Jazz Awards in 1989, 1991 and 1993 and was awarded an MBE just prior to his death. Sadly the year 2000 witnessed Kenny's death, yet many continue to look on his life with an overwhelming sense of pride. Like every good musician Kenny Baker spent his life enjoying his music and providing inspiration for the young musicians of today and thus left behind a valuable legacy.

Another secret that Withernsea gives home to is the fact that there is a novel named 'South Riding' which is based upon the town and its inhabitants. In 1934, writer Winifred Holtby stayed in Withernsea from mid-March to early June, in this period she gathered material for what was to be one of her

Fame at Last

best selling novels 'South Riding.' During her residence in the town she stayed at Delma, now known as 27 Waxholme Road. 'Kiplington' the town in the novel identifies to Withernsea in many ways, in addition to a scenic resemblance of the area, certain characters hint towards some of the towns more well known residents. Unfortunately, Holtby did not live long enough to see the success of her novel and died in 1935, one month after its completion. It was published in 1936 and became an immediate best seller and in 1937 the novel won the James Tait Black Memorial Prize. In recent years the novel was resurrected in the form of a T.V. series, Dorothy Tutin and Nigel Davenport starred in the Yorkshire Television production of 'South Riding'. To remember Holtby's fascinating achievement a commemorative plaque is on display at 27 Waxholme Road.

Despite numerous brushes with fame, the town continues to bury its secrets in the deepest depths of the past. Not boasting its tale, but leaving it to be unearthed by those who refuse to be caught up in the flurry of their daily lives, and those who care to take the time.

Chapter 9

Films, Films, Films

It was just before the First World War when the cinema revolution hit Withernsea. The 'Kinema,' a name many believed to be spelt incorrectly, was situated in central Queen Street and a small fee of 1 penny was enough to entitle the eager audience to a seat in the front and back stalls, however, this entrance fee was reduced if an empty jam jar was taken along for recycling. A seat in the balcony cost 2 pence but those were often taken up by the towns more affluent children. Nevertheless, a trip to the cinema was a form of escapism. Regardless of status, the voyeuristic experience the cinema offered sent adrenalin pumping, tensions increased as children watched their favourite heroes get into awfully tedious situations, and the added frustration of the cliff hanger was determined to have the audience back the next weekend to discover the outcome. The 'Kinema' mainly catered for children, with its highly popular Saturday matinees consisting of a cartoon, usually the old favourite Mickey Mouse, and then the eagerly awaited main feature, it was a sure hit. This main feature was often a serial which would span over a six week period, usually a tale of 'Cowboys and Indian's.' With the slick storylines the cinema had to offer, audience participation was inevitable, knuckles whitened as excited the children clung to their seats, every now and again shouting to warn of danger behind. However, the Christmas matinee was an extra special event enjoyed by all, each child, in addition to their admittance to the screening, also received an orange, an apple and a bag of sweets.

In 1929 Withernsea's second cinema was opened containing enough room to seat 720 people, it was originally named 'The Select' and was situated on the site of the Central Hall. It changed it's name to the 'Savoy' in 1931. The 'Savoy' was managed by Louis Surr and, in comparison to the 'Kinema' it was extremely modern. Its comfortable seats and modern decor made it attractive to the courting couples of the town and thus it became the 'fashionable' place to be seen in. The prices of the seats were higher than those of the 'Kinema,' so it was not unusual for the audience to consist mainly of adults.

The 'Cosy,' Withernsea's third cinema, opened just after the Second World War, it had fewer seats than the 'Select,' 666 in comparison to 720. It also had no balcony, so all seating was arranged on the ground floor, the films it screened were more suited to adult tastes. Thus, with three cinemas up and running, Withernsea had screenings to cater for all, yet this did not last forever. The period between 1950 and 1960 saw a rapid decline of the cinema as a popular form of entertainment. The dilemma was a result of the boycott of

Films, Films, Films

British cinemas by American film distributors, this occurred in 1948 due to a balance of payment crisis. As a result of this reissues filled the screen for over a year. However, the most potent reason for a lack of interest in the Cinema was the marriage boom which took place after the war, resulting in families staying at home to raise the children.

The 'Kinema' was the first to close in the 1960's, it was transformed into an amusement arcade. The 'Savoy' burnt down on the 24th March 1962. And finally the 'Cosy' closed on the 31st December 1974 and is now known as the Victorian Tavern situated along Queen Street. This marked the end of the Cinema revolution of Withernsea.

Chapter 10

All the Fun of the Fair

As Withernsea's popularity as a tourist resort increased, so did its entertainment facilities. Numerous beach performances, dance halls and general entertainment facilities such as swings and roundabouts gradually evolved in the town to welcome the new rush of visitors. A public salt-water pool was opened in July 1911, again promoting the revolutionary health giving seawater as prescribed by Sir John Floyer and Dr Richard Russel. It was located to the southern side of the town, in close proximity to the sea, which provided the pool with a constant supply of water. The pool, over 100 feet long and 45 feet wide was used by residents and tourists alike.

However, one of the most popular forms of entertainment was provided by Caitlin's Pierrots, who amused tourists with their daily beach performances from the summer of 1905. Many acts strove to follow in their footsteps, including the Merry Mascots and the First Army Follies, all of whom developed their own unique acting style. Many performances were also seen in the frequent talent shows, which offered the general public the chance to try their hand at entertaining, the results of which were sometimes astounding! An example of this is Bunny Doyle, a Hull Comedian, who made his debut on Withernsea beach after visiting the resort on holiday and winning a talent contest. It was the thrill of the experience which resulted in the ambitious young man seriously considering a future career alongside the Pierrots. Shortly after, Doyle made his first professional appearance at the Bijou music hall in Hull, later going on to tour the Northern Halls.

Another aspiring Pierrot who graced the coastline with his presence was Hull comedian, Dicky Henderson, he performed on the beach, making one of his first professional appearances with the Pierrots. During the 1920's 'The Yorkshire Comedian' stormed the USA with his humorous antics, making such an impact that he broke into the movie industry, being in demand by producers such as the Warner Brothers. Yet his heart still remained with the Pierrots, and, deciding that America wasn't for him, he returned to England, captivating his fellow Englishmen with his return to his native town.

Entertainment was not an activity reserved solely for the seafront; many indoor venues were also located within the town, such as the Unity Hall, the Pier Hotel, and the Floral Hall, to name but a handful. The Unity Hall played host to various shows, it was built in 1915 and formed part of the Withernsea Co-operative Society's premises in Queen Street south. The Pier Hotel assembly rooms also provided entertainment facilities but these burned down in 1913

All the Fun of the Fair

and a new entertainment venue had to be quickly found. However, the onset of the First World War saw the once bustling and lively resort transformed as a deathly hush crept over the town, and for the first time fears arose concerning the future of the tourist resort. Yet this blip didn't last for long and in the early 1920's there was a revival in the Pierrot performances and concert parties. By this time many entertainers were now ex-servicemen, unemployed and without any opportunity of work. Not giving up hope, they grouped together forming their own acts and entertaining the public in every type of venue from places as diverse as the London stage to small venues such as tourist resorts. An especially unusual performance named the First Army Follies, performed in the town and claimed "Every artiste a soldier, every soldier an artiste and every Lady a Gentleman." Their act was similar to that of female impersonators today, with the exception that they provided family entertainment. The public loved them and flocked to see the unusual actors, whose act was somewhat of a novelty.

Another novel show, again in popular demand with the public was the Lavender club. Returning to the town time after time and presented by Edgar Taylor, a dancer and comedian, the original show which was designed to keep the audience involved throughout lived up to its claim. In a show that provided non-stop entertainment, inclusive not only of singing but also tinged with dancing, comedy and a wide variety of sketches, it was clearly a performance that was not thrown together, but was delivered with a high degree of professionalism.

However the year of 1921 hinted at the future direction entertainment was to take, when the first amusement arcade was opened in the former lifeboat house on Seaside Road. Yet this change was not to take place until future decades and in 1925 the Central Hall was built in Queen Street south. Not only did this new hall compensate for the loss of the Pier Hotel Assembly Rooms, but it also provided a useful amenity for the general public in which meetings could be housed. But perhaps one of the most popular places of entertainment was the Floral Hall, which hosted performances from Vaudeville shows to the Pierrots. The Floral Hall, located at the south end of Pier Road, provided an arena for concerts with seating to suffice 700. Surprisingly, an older construction was still a favourite with performers, the Pier Towers remained one of the most popular backdrops for many shows, playing host to numerous performances.

In addition to the shows that the town had to offer, there were many smaller entertainment facilities. These included roundabouts and swings which, when

Beneath the Guiding Light

the weather permitted, were set up on the beach, a golf course, bowling green, roller-skating rink, and not to forget the English tradition of donkey rides along the beach. There were also many competitive entertainments within which the tourists could become involved, these included Swimming Galas, Regattas and Exhibitions. All of these were put to full use by the crowds who surged into the town during the summer period. In the months of June, July and August of 1925 almost 200,000 passengers travelled by rail from Hull to Withernsea and it seemed that the town had become fully established as a, perhaps not so quiet, family seaside resort.

It was around this time that one of the town's most prevalent traditions, the Withernsea Carnival, was coined. The celebrations spanned for a week and during these days everyone, residents and tourists alike, dressed up in outrageous costumes and enjoyed the celebrations. Those who weren't quite as eager to join in with the activities could sit and watch the processions from one of the numerous pleasant lawns. These lawns were the pride of the town, well stocked with flowers, they required constant upkeep, but for many the final result was well worth the continual commitment. Not only could people

Live shows were extremely popular with residents and tourists alike. An indoor venue was always on standby in case the weather took a turn for the worse.

All the Fun of the Fair

sit in these areas and observe the flurry of activity, but they could also enjoy a constant supply of refreshments from the stalls around the Pier Towers which were well stocked with ice cream and jugs of tea. And thus while the procession bustled by, the onlookers could relax in perfect bliss. Even when the Carnival wasn't taking place, many people used the lawns, perhaps listening to the town band, which was always in regular attendance. The band turned out on every and any occasion, especially Sundays, and in their smart blue uniforms they were the pride of Withernsea. One memorable member of the band was Kenny Baker, who learnt to play the trumpet with the band, only to go on to become Britain's leading trumpeter.

Another memorable entertainer was Irene Lawson, who recently received a BEM (British Empire Medal) for her influential role in the world of dancing. In 1933, when still a teenager, she founded the 'Reldene' School of Dancing, the name an anagram of her first place of employment, 'Needlers' of Hull. In the same year she performed her first show at the Unity Hall. From this point Irene's career involved a succession of achievements, a time from which she never looked back. Consistently providing dancers for the summer shows, Irene helped many young dancers achieve their dream. Her shows were highly successful and provided many hours of entertainment for both visitors and townsfolk alike, she continued to produce shows on a yearly basis until her retirement in 1996, giving the money raised to local charities.

Yet when the hustle and bustle of the summer months had passed, the town's residents enjoyed having the place to themselves. Although the tourist season only lasted approximately 8-9 weeks, a time during which it was crucial for the performers and railway companies to make the majority of their yearly profit, when the tourists left, Withernsea took on the appearance of a Ghost-Town. Nevertheless, the resident's enjoyed the peace and quiet brought on by the onset of the winter period, they could indulge in the entertainment facilities at their own free will, without having to force their way through crowded streets. And although people still came from Hull to attend the Saturday night dances, local inhabitants could not fail to enjoy unlimited usage of the town's bowling green, golf course, skating rink, and even an occasional stroll along the deserted beach.

Despite the long enjoyed period of desertion, the activity of the summer months never failed to return. And even though the summer sometimes brought change, it often worked out for the best. This was the case in the 1930's when the popularity of roller-skating began to decline. Yet despite this decline the Rink, adjoining the station, remained the focal point of entertainment. It was

Beneath the Guiding Light

turned into a huge stage and mainly catered for Saturday night dances which were held for the youngsters of the town. A bitter blow struck the community when the place burned down in the late 1930's, leaving only a few dance venues, which in the eyes of the youngsters were nothing in comparison to the Skating Rink. This disappointment soon turned to joy when it was quickly replaced by the Grand Pavilion. With its sprung maple dance-floor, the Grand Pavilion soon became recognised as the largest and finest dancehall on the East Coast, thus becoming the pride of Withernsea. With it's reputation spreading far and wide, not only did the Pavilion enhance the towns status, but it also overtook the Floral Hall with it's popularity, ensuring that the building was not greatly missed when it burnt down. The Grand Pavilion was the brainchild of Cecil Rhodes, a local fruit merchant and resident of the town, at first his idea received much opposition and thus, as a recognition of his determination in the face of adversity, a plaque in his honour was displayed at the front entrance of the hall.

Sadly, the Second World War saw the temporary closure of seaside resorts, and for many, was to mark the beginning of a drastic change in the traditional family holiday. The splitting up of families showed the emotionally turbulent period for what it was, this was echoed by the drastic action of the wiring off of beaches. When the war ended, Withernsea was not in an unfamiliar state to the rest of the country, it had emerged rundown and shabby, resonating the devastation that the war had spread. Rehabilitation of the town seemed an impossibility, due to a lack of money and the inability to obtain the required materials, many of which had been used up during the war, the country was in a state of injury. However, after a slow and painful battle, the town was gradually restored and by the 1950's Withernsea was again on its feet as a tourist resort. It was after the Second World War that the Grand Pavilion enjoyed its main period of success, often filled to its capacity of 1000 dancers. It welcomed world renown dance orchestras such as Victor Sylvester, Edmundo Ross and Joe Loss, all of whom were greeted by trainloads of people from Hull and the surrounding villages. Trains were also scheduled accordingly for Saturday nights, with the last train of the day leaving as the dances ended. During this period the venue was also popular with local organisations who frequently attended the highly praised dinner dances the Grand Pavilion offered. In more recent times it played host to many famous bands including Def Leppard, Iron Maiden, Slade and Jam. It was only after the dance boom that attendances began to fall and the magnificent venue began to decline.

Not surprisingly, the post war period saw a drastic change in seaside entertainment, the once popular acts such as the Pierrots and other seaside

All the Fun of the Fair

shows failed to return, leaving the sea front in a state of desertion. The roundabouts and various beach entertainments that were once in high demand were now obsolete and for many the innocence of the days gone by had been violated, a status that could never be regained. To the surprise of many and despite the odds, there was one group that emerged full of vitality. The Hollym Follies entertained tourists and were the closest act to the old-fashioned Pierrot shows. The group formed in 1962, originally intending their shows to be performed at the Women's Institute Spurn Group Rally, little did they know that this was just the beginning of their long and prosperous career. After the buzz of the first show, the group decided that they enjoyed performing to such an extent that they would continue with their light-hearted ways. Performing regular shows in Withernsea, even starring at the Grand Pavilion, the group donated all proceeds to charity and continued with their charitable ways until the year of 1980, when they disbanded due to a depletion in numbers. Thus, one of the final entertainment shows closed its door on the town.

Despite attempts to keep up a brave face, the town just wasn't the same after the war. Although visitors from Hull still crowded to the resort at weekend's no one could fail to notice that tastes had changed. It was the amusement arcades and bingo halls that now attracted people, and with the onset of the era of gambling, many were certain that the innocence of the good old days really had been lost. Yet the final blow hit the town hard when the 'Beeching Axe' fell in 1964 and the railway was doomed to closure, taking with it many happy memories of the town. Now with the bustle and chatter replaced by electronic melodies, for many, Withernsea is not the town that it once was. Yet many tourists return on a yearly basis, to walk down memory lane, attempting to recapture the nostalgia that remains ensnared within the town.

Bibliography

Baker Paul, Wooden Boats and Men of Steel: The Withernsea Lifeboats 1862-1913, A. E. Lunn.

Chapman Mave and Ben, The Pierrots of the Yorkshire Coast, Hutton Press, 1988.

Craven Martin, The Hull to Withernsea Railway 1854-1964, 1997.

Easdown Martin, Piers of Disaster, Hutton Press, 1996.

Fisher Kathleen, Hollym, Highgate Publications, 1990.

Miles G. T. J, A History of Withernsea, A. Brown & Sons Ltd, 1911.

Preedy Bob, Remembering the Old Cinemas of Humberside, Amadeus Press Ltd, 1988.

Sheppard Thomas, The Lost Towns of the Yorkshire Coast, Mr Pye Books, 1986.

Summer Ian and Margaret, Holderness, Alan Sutton Publishing Ltd, 1995.

Waters G. C, Withernsea and its Schools, A. E. Lunn, 1978.

Whitehead John, Withernsea, Highgate Publications, 1998.

Whittaker Jack, Withernsea in Old Picture Postcards, European Library.